FINAL *Wishes*

A Journal for Reflections on Life and Guidance for Settling Your Affairs

AMY LEVINE

ROCK POINT

With the new day comes new strength and new thoughts.

Eleanor Roosevelt

Contents

PERSONAL DETAILS

OWNER OF THIS BOOK

NAME

First ....

Middle ....

Last ....

Nickname (What do people call you?) ....

DATE OF BIRTH

Month .... Day .... Year ....

PLACE OF BIRTH

Town/City .... State .... Country ....

CURRENT ADDRESS

Street ....

Town/City .... State ....

NEXT OF KIN

Name ....

Phone .... Email ....

Relationship:　　Partner ☐　　Spouse ☐　　Ex-Spouse ☐　　Ex-Partner ☐

Name ....

Phone .... Email ....

Relationship:　　Brother ☐　　Sister ☐　　Cousin ☐

EMERGENCY CONTACTS

Name ....

Phone .... Email ....

Relationship:　　Brother ☐　　Sister ☐　　Cousin ☐

Name ....

Phone .... Email ....

Relationship:　　Son ☐　　Daughter ☐　　Step-Son ☐　　Step-Daughter ☐

YOUR PETS

Name .... Dog ☐ Cat ☐ Bird ☐ Other (describe) ....

Name .... Dog ☐ Cat ☐ Bird ☐ Other (describe) ....

Name .... Dog ☐ Cat ☐ Bird ☐ Other (describe) ....

Name .... Dog ☐ Cat ☐ Bird ☐ Other (describe) ....

NOTES

....

....

....

....

....

....

....

....

....

....

Give light and people will find the way.

Ella Baker

HOW DID YOU GET YOUR NAME?

Many of us go through life with the same first, middle, and nicknames. Your name is how you have been known through the years, by acquaintances, colleagues, friends, and those you love. You have uttered, "my name is" thousands of times in your life. It was probably one of the first things you learned to spell and pronounce. Someone named you. Your name may follow a tradition in your family and reflect a window into your family history. You may have been named in honor of someone much admired and respected. Perhaps you do not know why you have your name, but have a story about the day you were born and how your name appeared on your birth certificate.

On the following pages, share what you know about your first name, your middle name, and your nickname. Who chose your name? Do you know why? Does it connect you to anyone else in your family? Is there a story of your naming?

PREPARING

BEING PREPARED

There is some reason you have picked up this book and are reading this page. Perhaps you are wondering what would happen if you suddenly became seriously ill and were unable to care for yourself as you do now. You may wonder who would take care of your plants, pay your bills, and be sure that those you care for are safe if you are unable to be there. At some point in life, we will all experience a life threatening illness that will lead to the end of our lives. It can happen at any time and at any age.

The information we do not share with others often relates to the daily routines that are important to who we are and how we like things done. Advance planning is simply making sure that your wishes for your health care treatment and financial, legal, and personal affairs are known. Taking control now will help ensure your voice is heard later by those entrusted to care for you and the life you are living. End of life is a stage of life.

We all want to be seen, known, and heard at all stages of life. We constantly share our thoughts and opinions with others. We learn from each other's experiences on what to do and formulate opinions and preferences for new experiences—sad, happy, and scary. How did we learn to ride a bike? How did we learn to not fall off? How did we learn to make coffee? And yet we are less forthcoming and willing to share when it comes to life-threatening illness, health care choices, dying, death, and what follows. We might ask each other about what to say or do when attending the funeral of someone of a different culture and spiritual tradition. In my experience, it rarely goes further.

My professional career has been working with people at the end stage of life. I represent what many people want to forget—the fact that we are mortal.

I believe that everything we experience is life, whatever stage we may be at on the continuum. I am happy to be sharing with you what I know, and I hope you will in turn share with others what you learn. Talking to each other helps us all decide what is right for us. We are all experts because we are human. I am hoping this book will help you not only to have a list of common documents to help people plan, but that it will help you formulate your preferences for the end stage of life.

Here is your opportunity to ensure that you are known, seen, and heard now and then. Those you entrust to care for you will be grateful not to have to guess your end-of-life wishes. It will ensure peace of mind for you and for those you leave behind.

WHY THIS BOOK IS DIFFERENT

I recognize that most people who are not in the field of health care or social services cannot possibly know what is available to them in order to prepare fully when facing a life-threatening illness.

This book provides a step-by-step guide that enables you to create an individualized plan that is right for you. There is no right or wrong when it comes to making these decisions. The most important thing is that your wishes are known, that people are knowledgeable about what those wishes are, and that those people can carry them out when the time comes.

Although this book is not a legal document and does not offer legal or medical advice, it provides a vital road map, guiding you to the commonly used forms and documents to help you gain control of your advance planning.

A greater understanding helps us all to arrive at the best choices for each of us when it comes to handling our financial, business, and personal affairs. An appreciation of the value of advance planning can also help us to express our preferences when it comes to life-sustaining medical treatment.

Ultimately, this book is all about you. This chance to reflect on who you are and how you want to be remembered is invaluable.

Life is a balance of holding on and letting go.

Rumi

HOW TO USE THIS BOOK AND WHAT TO EXPECT

Contacts: Throughout the book you will be filling in the names, phone numbers, and email addresses of key people in your life: your family, friends, accountant, and so on. Whatever method you use to store this information (cell phone, address book), you will need it.

Representatives: Key to planning, in advance of a serious illness or event, is to appoint people you trust to speak on your behalf for your medical care, financial and legal affairs, and the distribution of your possessions after you die.

Inquiry: For each section, there is a question to respond to as you would in a journal. Each prompt is applicable in some way to the section you are completing. These are carefully constructed to generate reflection and information about your beliefs, history, and what matters to you.

Narratives: Throughout the book, I share personal and professional experiences that illustrate the universality as well as the individuality of people's experiences at the end of life.

Revisions: I recommend that you review this book every three to six months in order to keep your contacts up to date, so write in pencil for these sections.

Book Location: You should keep this book in a safe place, yet accessible to those who need to find it. I suggest you inform those who will be consulting this book of its location.

Note Section: Each section ends with an additional page for adding anything that has not been covered, but that is important for others to know.

WHEN MY MOTHER DIED

My first story concerns one of the last conversations my sister and I had with our mother. I am grateful to her for her willingness to share her concerns, and grateful that we listened. My mother died unexpectedly one summer. She was well. Then she was not. Months before she died, my sister and I visited for the weekend. In the midst of catching up, my mother asked us each to get a piece of paper and a pen. "Make a list, girls, of the things you want from the house when I am dead." Startled, I felt uncomfortable. "You aren't going to die," we uttered emphatically. Here I was, a professional in end of life, and I was doubting my mother's life would end. Ever. I did not want to think about it.

"I mean it, you don't want to be sorting through stuff." I knew she was right. Reluctantly, we began jotting things down, glancing at each other, looking around the room. I felt uncomfortable. This was personal. "Remember the 'good dishes,' they are on the top shelf of the hall closet," she added. At one point, as my sister and I wondered out loud about the need to split up the good dishes, my mother quipped, "and don't drag me up to the plot in Massachusetts." She meant the family plot where my grandmother and grandfather were buried. Detailed instructions followed on where and how she wanted to be buried. "And, instead of a memorial, you can throw a party afterward. Invite everyone, that would be fun," she added cheerfully.

The weekend was filled with joy. We laughed a lot and listened to what irritated her about one neighbor and what she loved about playing chess with another, the book she was reading, and the short story she was writing. I left, as always, with a book that she had picked out for me to read.

When we got the call from the hospital, we knew what medical treatment she would want and what she would not want. We knew how to care for her life-ending illness and what her preferences were for all that came after. Her gift to us was that which we knew.

KEY DOCUMENTS

In preparation for your advance planning consider beginning with the key documents listed below. These offer you control over what medical care you prefer to receive, how your finances are handled, and to whom your property is distributed, and how. Consider these as examples of the kinds of documents available. Several, in particular those relating to health care decisions, are covered in greater depth in the health and well-being section of the book. In some cases, you may decide to consult an attorney to create these documents.

HEALTH CARE REPRESENTATIVE

A document that enables you to appoint someone (also known as an Agent or Proxy) you trust to express your wishes and make health care decisions for you, if you are unable to speak for yourself. Depending upon the document you are using, such as one issued by your state of residence, you will also be able to indicate a desire to receive, or not to receive, life-prolonging and sustaining medical interventions.

Have ☐   Want to Revise ☐   Need ☐

....
....
....

DURABLE POWER OF ATTORNEY FOR LEGAL/FINANCIAL DECISIONS

A document that enables you to appoint someone you trust to make decisions for you regarding your financial and legal matters at such time as you are unable to carry out these responsibilities yourself. This role can include paying bills that are current or are associated with care that you receive during an illness.

Have ☐   Want to Revise ☐   Need ☐

....
....
....

LAST WILL AND TESTAMENT

A legal document that communicates your wishes as to how your property (estate) is distributed after your death. The document outlines who will be given your personal possessions, property, money, and so on. It can also include wishes pertaining to the care of your dependents. You will need to appoint a person to settle your estate and carry out the wishes outlined in your last will and testament.

Have ☐　　　Want to Revise ☐　　　Need ☐

....

....

....

PASSWORD BOOK

A book that holds your passwords for social media accounts, computer access, email accounts, and so on.

Have ☐　　　Want to Replace ☐　　　Need ☐

....

....

....

Special Note: If you are currently the caregiver of someone who depends upon you, or your family includes pets, I recommend that you consult with your family and friends on planning for their care.

LOCATION OF IMPORTANT DOCUMENTS

Once you have completed your key documents, it will be essential for those entrusted to carry out your wishes to know where to find them. Keep a list of the places in which you store these, and other, important documents.

Special Note: We recommend that you give copies of the form in which you assign a health care representative and indicate your treatment preferences to both your health care representative and your doctor.

HEALTH CARE DIRECTIVE

....

DURABLE POWER OF ATTORNEY FOR LEGAL/FINANCIAL DECISIONS

....

LAST WILL AND TESTAMENT

....

MEDICAL INSURANCE CARD

....

SOCIAL SECURITY CARD

....

PASSWORD BOOK

....

PASSPORT

....

BANKING DOCUMENTS

....

DRIVER'S LICENSE

....

You are your best thing.

Toni Morrison

WHAT I WISH
I HAD KNOWN

Many of us have known someone who experienced a serious illness that kept them from working or socializing. We didn't ask, but possibly assumed, that they didn't want visitors. Others of us have known someone who died from an illness or as the result of an accident. Some of us have experienced the loss of parents and didn't get a chance to ask them something we wish we had known.

Think about an experience that you have had with someone you know who died. Is there something you wish you had known? Do you know someone who has been seriously ill and you are not sure what to say or do for them? Share your experience of the times you wanted to know something but didn't ask.

ADDITIONAL NOTES

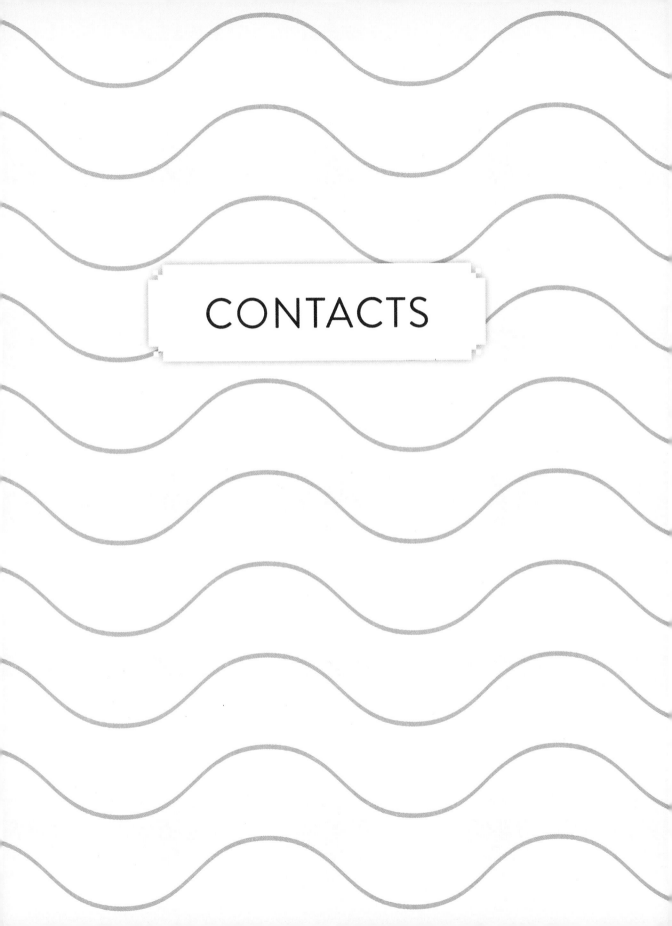

CONTACTS

KEY CONTACTS

Our world is made up of relationships. There are people we see daily, weekly, or even just occasionally. These relationships translate as the list of contacts we hold in our phones, in our email accounts, and in our address books.

Your contacts will be the places you shop for food and get your clothes dry-cleaned or laundered. They could include your gym or where you get your hair cut. Your contacts are your colleagues, your employer, your accountant, your attorney. Your contacts are your family members and close friends.

This section is for recording the names of your contacts and their contact information. Key contacts are the individuals and organizations that are part of your life and help to support your life. The information will ensure that bills are paid, belongings are found, and those you care about are kept up to date.

WHAT TO EXPECT

In this section you will be entering the names, phone numbers, and email addresses of all the individuals and organizations that are important to running your life: your key contacts.

The section is further divided into categories to include family, work, friends, spiritual/religious, pets, legal, medical, daily life, and entertainment. These categories may not cover everyone, so there is room at the end to add notes.

HOW TO BEGIN

You will need access to whatever source contains the names of your key contacts and their contact information.

I recommend that you go through this section in one sitting and fill in the names. If in doubt about a phone number or email address you can go back to fill it in later on.

Not everyone has email and in some cases it is not the best way for that person or organization to be contacted. You are the one who knows best.

Fill in what is current and relevant to your life as it is right now. There are areas to place check marks to indicate the relationship of the person you list. The lists are fairly comprehensive, but there will likely be something or someone who does not fit into the list. Please use the section for additional notes in such instances. You can also use it as your own personal action list of things you need to return to in order to complete the information.

WHAT MY MOTHER FORGOT TO TELL US

During the weekend my sister and I spent with my mother before she died, my mother shared a lot. She shared with us what she cared about and what was on her mind and in her heart. We knew what to do with her belongings and who would get her possessions. She shared what she believed, for her, was the quality of life and medical care she wanted, and what she didn't want if we were told there was no hope for her to live life how she wanted.

We grew up in the home that she lived in until she died. The rooms changed seasonally. During the summer, a rug appeared in the living room and curtains on the windows. During the winter, a different rug replaced the "summer" rug and another set of curtains appeared. As children we would balance ourselves on what I now realize was the winter rug wrapped in brown paper, which lined the wall in the hallway between the living room and kitchen in summer. The closets were small but there was always room for our coats and they would be there when we needed them. After my mother died we journeyed up ladders to reach the highest shelves of forgotten memories. We found the "good" dishes and rediscovered family photographs. Winter could not be found—no rug, no curtains, no coats. The sorting took several months. The mail was forwarded and a bill appeared from a storage cleaners for a rug, a set of curtains, and two women's coats. Our childhood winters had reappeared.

A MEMORY
My Childhood Best Friend

What is the first thought that comes to mind about a best friend you had when you were a child? Possibly you are thinking about someone from elementary school or a pal in your community. Share the memories you have about that friend.

FAMILY

PARTNER

Name ....

Relationship: Partner ☐   Spouse ☐   Ex-Spouse ☐   Ex-Partner ☐

Phone .... Email ....

Name ....

Relationship: Partner ☐   Spouse ☐   Ex-Spouse ☐   Ex-Partner ☐

Phone .... Email ....

Name ....

Relationship: Partner ☐   Spouse ☐   Ex-Spouse ☐   Ex-Partner ☐

Phone .... Email ....

CHILDREN

Name ....

Relationship: Son ☐   Daughter ☐   Step-Son ☐   Step-Daughter ☐

Phone .... Email ....

Name ....

Relationship: Son ☐   Daughter ☐   Step-Son ☐   Step-Daughter ☐

Phone .... Email ....

Name ....

Relationship: Son ☐   Daughter ☐   Step-Son ☐   Step-Daughter ☐

Phone .... Email ....

Name ....

Relationship: Son ☐   Daughter ☐   Step-Son ☐   Step-Daughter ☐

Phone .... Email ....

Name ....

Relationship: Son ☐   Daughter ☐   Step-Son ☐   Step-Daughter ☐

Phone .... Email ....

GRANDCHILDREN

Name ....

Relationship: Grandson ☐   Granddaughter ☐

Phone .... Email ....

Name ....

Relationship: Grandson ☐   Granddaughter ☐

Phone .... Email ....

Name ....

Relationship: Grandson ☐   Granddaughter ☐

Phone .... Email ....

Name ....

Relationship: Grandson ☐   Granddaughter ☐

Phone .... Email ....

Name ....

Relationship: Grandson ☐   Granddaughter ☐

Phone .... Email ....

SIBLINGS

Name ....

Relationship: Brother ☐   Sister ☐

Phone .... Email ....

Name ....

Relationship: Brother ☐   Sister ☐

Phone .... Email ....

Name ....

Relationship: Brother ☐   Sister ☐

Phone .... Email ....

Name ....

Relationship:　　Brother ☐　　Sister ☐

Phone .... Email ....

Name ....

Relationship:　　Brother ☐　　Sister ☐

Phone .... Email ....

Name ....

Relationship:　　Brother ☐　　Sister ☐

Phone .... Email ....

COUSINS

Name ....

Phone .... Email ....

Name ....

Phone .... Email ....

Name ....

Phone .... Email ....

Name ....

Phone .... Email ....

Name ....

Phone .... Email ....

Name ....

Phone .... Email ....

Name ....

Phone .... Email ....

NIECES AND NEPHEWS

Name ....

Relationship: Niece ☐   Nephew ☐

Phone .... Email ....

Name ....

Relationship: Niece ☐   Nephew ☐

Phone .... Email ....

Name ....

Relationship: Niece ☐   Nephew ☐

Phone .... Email ....

Name ....

Relationship: Niece ☐   Nephew ☐

Phone .... Email ....

Name ....

Relationship: Niece ☐   Nephew ☐

Phone .... Email ....

Name ....

Relationship: Niece ☐   Nephew ☐

Phone .... Email ....

Name ....

Relationship: Niece ☐   Nephew ☐

Phone .... Email ....

Name ....

Relationship: Niece ☐   Nephew ☐

Phone .... Email ....

OTHER FAMILY MEMBERS

Name ....

Relationship ....

Phone .... Email ....

Name ....

Relationship ....

Phone .... Email ....

Name ....

Relationship ....

Phone .... Email ....

Name ....

Relationship ....

Phone .... Email ....

Name ....

Relationship ....

Phone .... Email ....

Name ....

Relationship ....

Phone .... Email ....

Name ....

Relationship ....

Phone .... Email ....

Name ....

Relationship ....

Phone .... Email ....

Name ....

Relationship ....

Phone .... Email ....

There is no remedy for love but to love more.

Henry David Thoreau

FRIENDSHIPS

FRIENDS

Name ....

Phone .... Email ....

Name ....

Phone .... Email ....

Name ....

Phone .... Email ....

Name ....

Phone .... Email ....

Name ....

Phone .... Email ....

Name ....

Phone .... Email ....

Name ....

Phone .... Email ....

Name ....

Phone .... Email ....

Name ....

Phone .... Email ....

Name ....

Phone .... Email ....

Name ....

Phone .... Email ....

Name ....

Phone .... Email ....

Name ....

Phone .... Email ....

Name ....

Phone .... Email ....

Name ....

Phone .... Email ....

Name ....

Phone .... Email ....

Name ....

Phone .... Email ....

Name ....

Phone .... Email ....

Name ....

Phone .... Email ....

NEIGHBORS

Name ....

Phone .... Email ....

Name ....

Phone .... Email ....

Name ....

Phone .... Email ....

Name ....

Phone .... Email ....

WORK AND BUSINESS

EMPLOYER

Name ....

Phone .... Email ....

Name ....

Phone .... Email ....

WORK COLLEAGUES

Name ....

Phone .... Email ....

Name ....

Phone .... Email ....

Name ....

Phone .... Email ....

Name ....

Phone .... Email ....

BUSINESS PARTNERS

Name ....

Phone .... Email ....

Name ....

Phone .... Email ....

Name ....

Phone .... Email ....

Name ....

Phone .... Email ....

SPIRITUAL AND RELIGIOUS

SPIRITUAL TEACHER

Name ....

Phone .... Email ....

SPIRITUAL TEACHER

Name ....

Phone .... Email ....

RELIGIOUS TEACHER

Name ....

Phone .... Email ....

RELIGIOUS LEADER

Name ....

Phone .... Email ....

PLACE OF WORSHIP

Name ....

Phone .... Email ....

Name ....

Phone .... Email ....

PETS

VETERINARIAN

Phone .... Email ....

PET SITTER

Phone .... Email ....

GROOMING

Phone .... Email ....

Nothing can dim the light that shines from within.

Maya Angelou

LEGAL AND FINANCIAL

ATTORNEY

....

Phone .... Email ....

FINANCIAL ADVISOR

....

Phone .... Email ....

ACCOUNTANT

....

Phone .... Email ....

DURABLE POWER OF ATTORNEY

LEGAL POWER OF ATTORNEY

....

Phone .... Email ....

EXECUTOR (LAST WILL & TESTAMENT)

....

Phone .... Email ....

MEDICAL

HEALTH CARE REPRESENTATIVE (AGENT/PROXY)

....

Phone .... Email ....

PRIMARY DOCTOR

....

Phone .... Email ....

DENTIST

....

Phone .... Email ....

PSYCHIATRIST

....

Phone .... Email ....

COUNSELOR

....

Phone .... Email ....

PHARMACY

....

Phone .... Email ....

OPTICIAN

....

Phone .... Email ....

OTHER MEDICAL PROVIDERS

....

Phone .... Email ....

....

Phone .... Email ....

....

Phone .... Email ....

....

Phone .... Email ....

You are never too old to set another goal, or to dream a new dream.

C.S. Lewis

DAILY LIFE

GAS/ELECTRIC COMPANY

....

Phone .... Email ....

WATER COMPANY

....

Phone .... Email ....

CABLE/TV COMPANY

....

Phone .... Email ....

INTERNET COMPANY

....

Phone .... Email ....

LANDLINE PHONE COMPANY

....

Phone .... Email ....

CELL PHONE COMPANY

....

Phone .... Email ....

STORAGE UNIT

....

Phone .... Email ....

DRY-CLEANER

....

Phone .... Email ....

GROCERY STORE

....

Phone .... Email ....

CAR MECHANIC

....

Phone .... Email ....

GARAGE

....

Phone .... Email ....

PLUMBER

....

Phone .... Email ....

ELECTRICIAN

....

Phone .... Email ....

COMPUTER TECHNICIAN

....

Phone .... Email ....

ONLINE ACCOUNTS

COMPUTER ACCESS

PERSONAL

Login ....

Password ....

WORK

Login ....

Password ....

SOCIAL MEDIA

Facebook ☐   Twitter ☐   Instagram ☐   Other ....

Login ....

Password ....

Facebook ☐   Twitter ☐   Instagram ☐   Other ....

Login ....

Password ....

Facebook ☐   Twitter ☐   Instagram ☐   Other ....

Login ....

Password ....

Facebook ☐   Twitter ☐   Instagram ☐   Other ....

Login ....

Password ....

Facebook ☐   Twitter ☐   Instagram ☐   Other ....

Login ....

Password ....

Facebook ☐   Twitter ☐   Instagram ☐   Other ....

Login ....

Password ....

OTHER ACCOUNTS

Account ....

Login ....

Password ....

Account ....

Login ....

Password ....

Account ....

Login ....

Password ....

Account ....

Login ....

Password ....

Account ....

Login ....

Password ....

Account ....

Login ....

Password ....

Account ....

Login ....

Password ....

Account ....

Login ....

Password ....

ENTERTAINMENT

THEATER TICKET/SUBSCRIPTIONS

....

....

CONCERT TICKET/SUBSCRIPTIONS

....

....

MAGAZINE SUBSCRIPTIONS

....

....

GYM MEMBERSHIP

....

....

SPORTING EVENTS TICKET/SUBSCRIPTIONS

....

....

OTHER

....

....

You only live once, but if you do it right, once is enough.

Mae West

WHAT DO YOU DO TO HAVE FUN?

We experience fun throughout our lives. Thinking about such times always brings a smile to the face. Some of us associate fun with things that make us laugh. Others think of childhood memories. Fun can involve other people or be something that we experience alone. For some of us it means discovering something new—reading a new book, listening to music, or watching a movie or TV show. Or perhaps it involves an activity, sport, or game. Fun doesn't always mean big and loud, but can be small and quiet. It comes in all shapes and sizes.

Above all, fun is personal. You know when you are having fun. What would be a great day for you? Think about the things you do that you find fun? Why are they so? What fun childhood memories do you have? What are your memories of having fun as a teenager or young adult? Share at least five activities that you enjoy now or have enjoyed in the past. Add to the list. Keep going.

ADDITIONAL NOTES

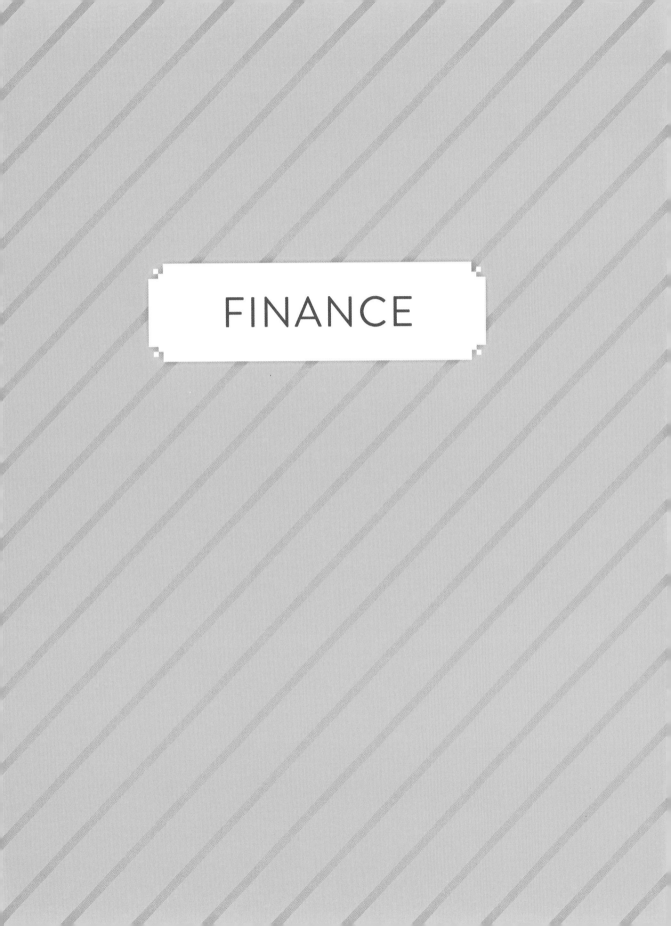

FINANCE

FINANCIAL INFORMATION

Finance is a term most commonly associated with managing money in large quantities. For this section, we use it to cover the ways in which we buy, sell, protect, and grow our money. We purchase in many ways. Checks and debit cards draw currency out of banks that keep our money safe. Credit cards allow us to spend now and pay later. We earn our money by working different jobs and have different professions. Some of us enjoy our work; some of us don't and are eager to take retirement pensions so we can do the things we really enjoy doing. We inherit money and donate money to charitable organizations that help others and contribute to our planet. Money means so much more than dollars and cents.

WHAT TO EXPECT

Some of us are used to talking about money. Others are less in the habit of talking about it and feel uncomfortable when others do. They consider it a private matter. Tax time may be the only time many of us undertake a thorough review of our finances. Money can be a source of both worry and joy. There are people who play the lottery for fun and imagine how they will spend their winnings.

This section does not ask you to reveal dollar amounts. Instead, you are being asked to provide information on where you keep your money, the ways in which you grow it, and how you use it to protect yourself. You will be asked to list businesses that you own, for example. You will also have an opportunity to give a full picture of the organizations and institutions that support your health and well-being.

Some of the information may appear repetitive. It is. This book is designed in such a way that information is easily accessible to those you have entrusted to take care of your affairs. This section is divided into categories: banking, retirement benefits, legal and financial representatives, insurance coverage, business ownership, and charities.

There's power in allowing yourself to be known and heard, in owning your unique story, in using your authentic voice.

Michelle Obama

HOW TO BEGIN

To complete this section, you will need access to the names and addresses of your financial institutions, insurance companies, and business associates and representatives. There are areas to place check marks to indicate what type of an account or coverage exists with a given organization. I recommend that you go through this section in one sitting and fill in all the information that you readily know or have access to. If in doubt about anything, you can go back to fill it in later on. Fill in what is current and relevant to your life as it is right now.

Use the additional notes page at the end of this section to list anything that isn't included. You can also use it as your own personal action list of things you need to return to in order to complete the information.

Don't judge each day by the harvest you reap but by the seeds that you plant.

Robert Louis Stevenson

COUNTING STARS

During my years working as a member of a hospice team, I met individuals from varying professions, cultures, spiritual traditions, and interests who were facing the last days, weeks, or months of their lives. I learned that everyone is an individual. I learned that I couldn't make assumptions based upon the demographic information I was given. An accountant by profession, Mr. B greeted me in his study where he sat at his desk and twirled around as I entered the room. He was dressed as if he was at work. But I was there to talk to him about finalizing his affairs and learn what he might need in his final days. I was there to begin to get to know him. Framed awards for professional excellence and plaques for civic duty filled the walls. A small statute of a golfer and a golf ball sat on a shelf along with photos. His career had spanned years and his speciality was money. We talked a long time. He began with the stories behind the awards, progessed to his passion for his profession, on to the crossword puzzles he was stumped by, and revealed a boyhood interest in astronomy. His illness progressed and a hospital bed replaced the desk that faced the study's picture window. One of my last visits was on a bright sunny summer's morning. I sat down next to the bed and he opened his eyes. I could hear the birds in the garden. Everything was green and welcoming. "Do you want to know what I am seeing?" he asked. With a gentle sense of awe, he began to describe planets and, with wonder, the stars that had zoomed in through the window the past few days and nights. "The stars keep coming, too many to count." I asked him if he felt frightened. With a soft smile, he simply answered, "I just saw Jupiter."

A MEMORY

Hidden Treasure

As a child did you ever find something that became your treasure?
A stone, a marble, a penny, a dollar—something that you kept in a box
or hidden—your secret? Share your memories of that treasured item.

BANKING

Bank Name .... Branch Location ....

☐ Savings Account   ☐ Checking Account   ☐ CD

☐ IRA   ☐ Safe Deposit Box

Personal Banker ....

Bank Name .... Branch Location ....

☐ Savings Account   ☐ Checking Account   ☐ CD

☐ IRA   ☐ Safe Deposit Box

Personal Banker ....

Bank Name .... Branch Location ....

☐ Savings Account   ☐ Checking Account   ☐ CD

☐ IRA   ☐ Safe Deposit Box

Personal Banker ....

Bank Name .... Branch Location ....

☐ Savings Account   ☐ Checking Account   ☐ CD

☐ IRA   ☐ Safe Deposit Box

Personal Banker ....

Bank Name .... Branch Location ....

☐ Savings Account   ☐ Checking Account   ☐ CD

☐ IRA   ☐ Safe Deposit Box

Personal Banker ....

Bank Name .... Branch Location ....

☐ Savings Account   ☐ Checking Account   ☐ CD

☐ IRA   ☐ Safe Deposit Box

Personal Banker ....

Bank Name .... Branch Location ....

☐ Savings Account ☐ Checking Account ☐ CD

☐ IRA ☐ Safe Deposit Box

Personal Banker ....

Bank Name .... Branch Location ....

☐ Savings Account ☐ Checking Account ☐ CD

☐ IRA ☐ Safe Deposit Box

Personal Banker ....

Bank Name .... Branch Location ....

☐ Savings Account ☐ Checking Account ☐ CD

☐ IRA ☐ Safe Deposit Box

Personal Banker ....

MORTGAGE

Bank Name .... Location ....

INVESTMENT COMPANY

Name .... Phone ....

INVESTMENT COMPANY

Name .... Phone ....

INVESTMENT DETAILS

....

....

....

....

....

....

RETIREMENT BENEFITS

EMPLOYER

....

Phone ....

UNION

....

Phone ....

INVESTMENT COMPANY

....

Phone ....

INVESTMENT COMPANY

....

Phone ....

SOCIAL SECURITY

Direct deposit ☐   Check ☐

It is not length of life, but depth of life.

Ralph Waldo Emerson

INSURANCE COVERAGE

Insurance Company ....

Type: Home ☐ Life ☐ Car ☐ Mortgage ☐ Other ....

Broker ....

Phone .... Email ....

Insurance Company ....

Type: Home ☐ Life ☐ Car ☐ Mortgage ☐ Other ....

Broker ....

Phone .... Email ....

Insurance Company ....

Type: Home ☐ Life ☐ Car ☐ Mortgage ☐ Other ....

Broker ....

Phone .... Email ....

Insurance Company ....

Type: Home ☐ Life ☐ Car ☐ Mortgage ☐ Other ....

Broker ....

Phone .... Email ....

Insurance Company ....

Type: Home ☐ Life ☐ Car ☐ Mortgage ☐ Other ....

Broker ....

Phone .... Email ....

Insurance Company ....

Type: Home ☐ Life ☐ Car ☐ Mortgage ☐ Other ....

Broker ....

Phone .... Email ....

GENERAL MEDICAL INSURANCE COVERAGE

Primary

Medicare ....

Medicare Number ....

Insurance Carrier Name ....

Insurance Number ....

Secondary

Insurance Carrier Name ....

Insurance Number ....

Dental Insurance Name ....

Insurance Number ....

Long-Term Care Insurance Name ....

Broker .... Phone ....

PROFESSIONAL INSURANCE

Company or Organization ....

Liability: Individual ☐   Practice ☐   General ☐

Company or Organization ....

Liability: Individual ☐   Practice ☐   General ☐

Power is the ability to do good things for others.

Brooke Astor

BUSINESS OWNERSHIP

BUSINESS NAMES

Name of Business ....

Partner Name ....

Phone .... Email ....

Name of Business ....

Partner Name ....

Phone .... Email ....

Name of Business ....

Partner Name ....

Phone .... Email ....

CHARITIES

Name ....

Phone .... Email ....

Name ....

Phone .... Email ....

Name ....

Phone .... Email ....

Name ....

Phone .... Email ....

WHAT DOES MONEY MEAN TO YOU?

There are many associations with the role money plays in our lives. It can make us feel worthy or unworthy. There can be a lack or an abundance. For some, achievement is measured by pay raises that come with promotions at work. We use money for good causes and to show our support of a mission, when the dollar amount does not matter. At times, we use it to thank someone or to express appreciation. We may have first experiences as children of saving pennies, playing with pennies, or receiving an allowance. Our experiences with money are unique.

What memory do you have of your first experience with money? A disappearing dollar in a magic show? An instructive talk with a parent about money? Do you remember opening your first bank account? What was that like? Who gave you the money to make your first deposit? Who escorted you? Share your memories of those early events.

ADDITIONAL NOTES

HEALTH &
WELL-BEING

MEDICAL CARE

Health and well-being is a lifelong pursuit for many of us. We decide on which doctors to see and what medicines to take. We form relationships with medical professionals and they guide us throughout our lives. We share our knowledge with each other about what works and what doesn't work. We exchange remedies and methods for preventing colds and offer advice on what to do when others get sick. We share the names of health care professionals, clinicians, and interventions. We seek information and learn about the options. We want to know what is right for us. We can choose now for later.

Well-being is knowing that you have planned in advance and have chosen someone you trust to know your medical treatment preferences. Well-being is knowing that the person you have appointed will discuss the options available in the future and be able to make the right decisions with the health care providers caring for you at the time.

WHAT TO EXPECT

Our individual experiences of medical care differ. Throughout our lives, many of us have visited doctors in their practices. Some of us have been patients and received care in a hospital. We have had the option to accept or refuse the care offered. It is our right.

When facing life-threatening illnesses we continue to have the right to accept or refuse the care offered, as do those acting on our behalf.

This section discusses the documents that enable you to name someone you trust to make decisions for you at a time when you are unable to speak for yourself. The details of future medical options cannot be predicted. However, decisions can be made now that will guide your representative regarding comfort and life-sustaining treatments. You have the opportunity now to begin thinking about what quality of life means to you.

The section is divided into three categories: medical details, medical representative, and care during hospitalization. You are not requested to enter details of your current or past medical history.

Nothing is worth more than laughter. It is strength to laugh and to abandon oneself, to be light.

Frida Kahlo

HOW TO BEGIN

To complete this section, you will need access to whatever source contains the names of your main health care providers and your attorney for medical decisions, if appointed. Listing the doctors that you see regularly will be very helpful to your care later.

I recommend that you go through this section in one sitting and fill in all the information that you readily know or have access to. If in doubt about anything, you can go back to fill it in later on. Fill in what is current and relevant to your life as it is right now.

Use the additional notes page at the end of this section to list anything that isn't included. You can also use it as your own personal action list of things you need to return to in order to complete the information.

A light heart lives long.

William Shakespeare

FOREVER CURIOUS

In my initial visits with Ms. M, she greeted me in her living room, sitting in front of a roaring fire in a large stone fireplace. She was surrounded by newspapers and neat piles of clippings. The clippings were stories on various topics she planned to share with family, friends, and colleagues. She enjoyed lively discussions and learning anything new. Occasionally, our conversations would be interrupted by a call or two. There were many visitors that overlapped with the hospice team's weekly visits. Ms. M considered us a part of her life and inquired as to our interests and life history. As her illness progressed into summer, she greeted me in her bedroom. Her glasses perched on her nose, she would look up from her newspapers, glance at the tennis game on television to catch the score, and then me. "Okay, what can you tell me about the world outside?" she quipped.

The hospital bed propped her up sufficiently to review the clippings for the day. I learned that she had loved to play tennis and had traveled the world. She loved to cook and before she became ill she'd had regular gatherings of friends to share meals with. The last time I visited, she was weakened and looked thinner, but was focused on learning a new language. Her dog lay at the foot of the bed content to be near her. That same day she spoke about her spiritual beliefs and the afterlife. She informed me that she had already made all of her burial and funeral arrangements.

"Any concerns or worries?" I asked, as I was in the habit of doing.

"About dying you mean?"

I nodded.

"I haven't ever done this before. I suppose it will be my last adventure." She smiled.

A MEMORY
Home From School

Did you ever stay home from school because you were sick? For some
of us it was a welcome escape from the classroom, while others were
eager to return to their classmates. What was it like for you? Share
your memories of the days you were home from school.

MEDICAL DETAILS

Are you a veteran?

Yes ☐   No ☐   Years of service ....

Are you entitled to VA benefits?

Yes ☐   No ☐   Don't Know ☐

Health Care Representative (Agent/Proxy) ....

Phone ....   Email ....

HEALTH INSURANCE

Location of Health Insurance Card ....

MEDICAL PROVIDERS

Primary Doctor ....

Phone ....

Other Medical Provider ....

Phone ....

Psychiatrist ....

Phone ....

Counselor ....

Phone ....

Preferred Hospital ....

Pharmacy ....

Phone ....

HEALTH CARE REPRESENTATIVE

The forms and terms that follow are tools you can use to name someone you trust to act on your behalf regarding health care treatment in the event of a terminal illness or traumatic event. These forms guide your representative as to the kinds of medical treatments you would want if you were not expected to make a full recovery. Keep in mind that there may be medical treatment and intervention options at that future date that cannot be determined today. In addition to whatever form you chose to appoint a representative, it is very important to discuss your wishes with them.

DEFINING TERMS

Several terms are used to describe the person you assign to make health care decisions for you in the event that you cannot. The following list is not exhaustive: health care agent, health care proxy, durable power of attorney for health care decisions.

Forms or documents in which you name this person as your representative include, but are not limited to: health care directive, health care proxy, living will.

Where to find a form:

Health Care Directive/Health Care Proxy

Check with the health department in your state of residence. The majority of states do not require an attorney to complete forms provided by your state.

Living Will

A living will can provide detailed instructions about health care decision-making. This document often requires an attorney.

DETERMINING WHAT IS RIGHT FOR YOU AT THE END OF LIFE

It can take time and thought to identify what quality of life means to you and how that could determine your care at the end of life. Some people find it helpful to consult with their faith/spiritual leaders, trusted doctors, and friends to help them formulate these decisions regarding end of life and life-sustaining medical treatments.

CHOOSING YOUR HEALTH CARE REPRESENTATIVE (AGENT/PROXY)

Your health care representative can be anyone you choose—a family member, friend, or anyone you trust to carry out your wishes. They must be willing to take on the role. It is important to share with that person what you value in life and your wishes regarding the provision or cessation of life-sustaining treatment. This knowledge will equip your representative with the ability to do their job with the utmost of confidence.

In the event that you have no one to appoint to be your health care representative, we suggest you call your local hospital's social work or chaplaincy department for assistance. They can refer you to someone (Advance Care Planner) who can guide you in expressing your wishes and preferences in a written document.

SHARING YOUR COMPLETED HEALTH CARE DIRECTIVE

It is important that your health care representative, your legal representative (if applicable), and your doctors have copies of your health care directive. The original should be accessible. In some states, if using a form provided by the health department, you may receive a wallet-sized document that lists the contact information of your representative.

ACTION LIST

I have appointed a health care representative

Yes ☐   No ☐   Scheduling ☐   Date to be completed ....

Name ....

Phone ....   Email ....

I have had a discussion with my health care representative, who knows my wishes

Yes ☐   No ☐   Scheduling ☐   Date for discussion ....

CARE DURING HOSPITALIZATION

WHAT'S IMPORTANT TO ME?

SPIRITUALITY/RELIGION

Important ☐   Not so important ☐   Not important ☐   Don't know ☐

VISITORS (OTHER THAN MEDICAL PERSONNEL)

Yes ☐   No ☐   Family ☐   Friends ☐   Other ....

I don't want to be alone ☐   I do want to be alone ☐   I don't know ☐

MUSIC

Yes ☐   No ☐   I don't know ☐

If yes, type of music:

Classical ☐   Spiritual/Religious ☐   Other ....

READ TO ME

Yes ☐   No ☐   I don't know ☐

If yes, what to read:

Poetry ☐   Spiritual/Religious ☐   Other ....

PLEASE ALSO NOTE ....

SOME OF MY CONCERNS

MY HOME / APARTMENT

Please take care of:

My pets ☐   My plants ☐   Other ....

OTHER CONCERNS ....

MY BEST VACATION

Bring to mind a vacation that you have taken that has stayed with you. Alternatively, how would the ideal vacation look to you now? A vacation day or week? Alone or with others? Far away or nearby? What comes to mind? Hone in on the details. What would you do? Where would you go? What would make it special to you? Share your vision of the perfect vacation.

ADDITIONAL NOTES

POSSESSIONS

BELONGINGS

Possessions. Your stuff. The things that surround you, the items you own and have the right to throw away, give away, or keep. We collect possessions both purposely and inadvertently. When we move, we discover stuff in drawers and closets we forgot we had. We shop in stores and online. We hunt things down and save our money to purchase things that give us pleasure. We have small things such as the kitchen can opener and big things such as the car or the house. We keep precious things hidden in drawers, we cherish items handed down for generations, we have favorite items for a wealth of reasons.

Reviewing your belongings now gives you the ability to make decisions on their disposition later on. You may own something that, when thinking about it, you would like to leave to someone. This is the time to take control. Deciding now relieves those in your life of the burden of guessing when you are not there to direct them.

WHAT TO EXPECT

A possession, something you own, can be of value for monetary or sentimental reasons, or for any number of other reasons. It can be an object that represents your family history, a trip, a special day, or a much-loved person. In the end you do not want it thrown out.

This section provides you with the opportunity to review your possessions and to consider their fate. You may discover something that would otherwise go unnoticed. You may want to show friends and family where your most prized possessions are located. This can be very helpful to them later.

This section does not serve as a legal document nor is it a place to name beneficiaries. Questions regarding your last will and testament should be directed to your attorney.

It's amazing how lovely common things become, if one only knows how to look at them.

Louisa May Alcott

HOW TO BEGIN

To complete this section, you will need available the names of and contact information for your executor, attorney, and anyone else tasked with taking care of your worldly affairs. You will also be asked to identify items that are relevant in the home and outside your home. This is not an exhaustive list.

I recommend that you go through this section in one sitting and fill in all the information that you readily know or have access to. If in doubt about anything you can go back to fill it in later on. Fill in what is current and relevant to your life as it is right now.

Use the additional notes page at the end of this section to list anything that isn't included. You can also use it as your own personal action list of things you need to return to in order to complete the information.

> **The best and most beautiful things in the world can not be seen or even touched.**
>
> Helen Keller

THE SHELF

I visited a family friend who had lived near me. I had entered her home hundreds of times. This time, it all felt different. She told me that she had been cleaning and, as a result, every surface was cluttered. She led me through the house as if she were giving me a tour for the first time. She took me to the bedroom and stopped in front of several large plastic boxes. She lifted the lid of each and explained their contents. Each box was neatly labeled. She opened drawers and showed me what was inside. We continued to her closet. Scarves were draped over the door. I had seen her wear them but didn't know she had designed them. We went into her small kitchen, where she talked about a memorable meal that she had created many years ago. I knew her for her salad dressing. As I was about to leave, she interrupted me and took me over to a dusty glass shelf in the living room. On the shelf were miniature, intricate sculptures in various sizes, shapes, and colors. Each represented a special event in her life, which she described to me. Some of them I was aware of, many I was not. I had overlooked this shelf all my life. Her gaze still on the objects, she swept her hand gently over each of them: "A life, a life," she mused.

A MEMORY

Something Lost

We lose possessions throughout our lives. Think of an early memory you have of "misplacing" or losing something that you cared about. Share the thoughts you had when you could not find this lost item.

LAST WILL AND TESTAMENT

This legal document communicates a person's wishes as to how their property (estate) is distributed after their death. It can also include wishes pertaining to the care of their dependents. Consult your attorney for guidance on drafting a last will and testament.

My Will Is Located ....

Attorney ....

Phone .... Email ....

Your executor is the person you appoint to settle your estate and carry out the wishes outlined in your last will and testament.

Executor ....

Phone .... Email ....

POSSESSIONS BY ROOM

KITCHEN

Recipe Books ....

Location ....

Dishes ....

Location ....

Glasses ....

Location ....

Shelf of Note ....

Location ....

Shelf of Note ....

Location ....

Drawer of Note ....

Location ....

Drawer of Note ....

Location ....

Other Items ....

Location ....

Other Items ....

Location ....

DINING ROOM

Cutlery ....

Location ....

Tablecloths/Napkins/Placemats ....

Location ....

Candlesticks ....

Location ....

Shelf of Note ....

Location ....

Shelf of Note ....

Location ....

Drawer of Note ....

Location ....

Drawer of Note ....

Location ....

Other Items ....

Location ....

Other Items ....

Location ....

LIVING ROOM

Cabinet ....

Location ....

Cabinet ....

Location ....

Tabletop Objects ....

Location ....

Shelf of Note ....

Location ....

Shelf of Note ....

Location ....

Drawer of Note ....

Location ....

Drawer of Note ....

Location ....

Other Items ....

Location ....

Other Items ....

Location ....

BEDROOM 1

Cabinet ....

Location ....

Cabinet ....

Location ....

Tabletop Objects ....

Location ....

Shelf of Note ....

Location ....

Shelf of Note ....

Location ....

Drawer of Note ....

Location ....

Drawer of Note ....

Location ....

Other Items ....

Location ....

Other Items ....

Location ....

BEDROOM 2

Cabinet ....

Location ....

Cabinet ....

Location ....

Tabletop Objects ....

Location ....

Shelf of Note ....

Location ....

Shelf of Note ....

Location ....

Drawer of Note ....

Location ....

Drawer of Note ....

Location ....

Other Items ....

Location ....

Other Items ....

Location ....

DEN/OFFICE

Inside House ☐   Outside House ☐   Location ....

Cabinet ....

Location ....

Cabinet ....

Location ....

Tabletop Objects ....

Location ....

Shelf of Note ....

Location ....

Shelf of Note ....

Location ....

Drawer of Note ....

Location ....

Drawer of Note ....

Location ....

Other Items ....

Location ....

Other Items ....

Location ....

BASEMENT

Cabinet ....

Location ....

Cabinet ....

Location ....

Box ....

Location ....

Box ....

Location ....

Shelf of Note ....

Location ....

Shelf of Note ....

Location ....

Drawer of Note ....

Location ....

Drawer of Note ....

Location ....

Other Items ....

Location ....

Other Items ....

Location ....

ATTIC

Box ....

Location ....

Box ....

Location ....

Shelf of Note ....

Location ....

Shelf of Note ....

Location ....

Drawer of Note ....

Location ....

Drawer of Note ....

Location ....

Other Items ....

Location ....

Other Items ....

Location ....

GARAGE

Box ....

Location ....

Box ....

Location ....

Shelf of Note ....

Location ....

Shelf of Note ....

Location ....

Drawer of Note ....

Location ....

Drawer of Note ....

Location ....

Other Items ....

Location ....

Other Items ....

Location ....

OTHER MEANINGFUL POSSESSIONS

COLLECTOR ITEMS

Coins ☐   Location ....

Stamps ☐   Location ....

Other ....

Location ....

Other ....

Location ....

Heirloom ....

Location ....

Heirloom ....

Location ....

Heirloom ....

Location ....

BOOKS

Collection ....

Location ....

Book ....

Location ....

Book ....

Location ....

Book ....

Location ....

Book ....

Location ....

Book ....

Location ....

ARTWORK AND OBJECTS

Collection ....

Location ....

Art ....

Location ....

Art ....

Location ....

Art ....

Location ....

Art ....

Location ....

Other ....

Location ....

Other ....

Location ....

LOCATED OUTSIDE MY HOME

Storage Unit ....

Location ....

Vehicle ....

Location ....

Garage ....

Location ....

Office Space ....

Location ....

Other ....

Location ....

Other ....

Location ....

Other ....

Location ....

Other ....

Location ....

Wherever you go, go with all your heart.

Confucius

TREASURED POSSESSIONS

Treasured possessions bring meaning to our lives. These objects may not be obvious to others, but all the same they are treasures, large and small. Your favorite possession might be something you purchased, an item you received as a gift, or something found. Some are passed down over time. Many possessions have monetary value, others none at all. For some of us it is the ring held safely inside a box in a drawer. For others it is a piano that stands in the home for all to see. Others still treasure a smooth stone that sits on a window ledge.

Think of at least five things that you care about and that bring you joy. Can you describe what makes each special to you? Make a note of how you came by each possession. Has it been in the family for generations? Did you purchase it? If so, when, where, and why? Did someone give it to you? If so, what was the occasion? What are the important things that you want people to know about these items?

ADDITIONAL NOTES

FUNERAL PLANS

IN MEMORY

A funeral is a ritual associated with death. It offers those who attend an opportunity to come together in honor of someone whose life has ended. Planning for a funeral is often a task that is out of mind and out of sight until we begin to feel our own mortality. It could be considered one of the last tasks in life: the last formal arrangement. Make decisions about your funeral now to ensure you get the funeral you want.

WHAT TO EXPECT

This section focuses on some of the decision-making you can do now for your funeral, memorial, and obituary. The options for burial have grown over the years and differ from state to state. Always check with your local authority for legal guidelines. This section lists the most basic of options and encourages you to conduct additional research to determine the best plan for you.

Perhaps you have already made arrangements for your funeral, in which case you can still enter the details here. By making as many decisions as you can now, you will bring comfort to those you leave behind. I encourage you to share this information with those who are tasked with carrying out your arrangements later on.

This section does not serve as a legal document nor as a funeral arrangement. It is a guide to some of the tasks associated with funeral and memorial planning.

HOW TO BEGIN

To complete this section, you will need the names and contact information for any burial arrangements you have made already.

I recommend that you go through this section in one sitting and fill in all the information that you readily know or have access to. If in doubt about anything, you can go back to fill it in later on. Fill in what is current and relevant to your life as it is right now.

Use the additional notes page at the end of this section to list anything that isn't included. You can also use it as your own personal action list of things you need to return to in order to complete the information.

THE SUIT

Mrs. G was a calm, know yourself kind of person. She had been a seamstress and came from a long line of women who had worked in the same profession. When I met her, she sat in a brown, upholstered lounge chair facing the door. All her neighbors knew her and many had a key to her house. They dropped by frequently with food and ran errands for her. Mrs G had an unshakable faith and told me she believed that everything occurs at the time that it is supposed to happen. She had survived many occurrences of cancer before but had no expectations of outliving this most recent recurrence. As her illness progressed, making it difficult for her to move around, she chose to spend her days mainly in her brown chair. During one of my visits, Mrs. G told me that, although she had made her funeral arrangements, she had not picked out an outfit.

"Outfit?" I asked.

"Yes, what I will be wearing when they bury me," she clarified.

She rose up out of her chair and, using her walker, led me to her closet. Mrs. G opened the closet door and ran her hand through the dresses and suits hanging neatly inside. She stopped at a light pink suit and touched the sleeve.

"Fine wool," she stated. "I made this suit you know. This is what I want to wear," she remarked as she sank back into her chair. That day I learned about silk linings and listened to memories of the finest garments Mrs. G created during her years as a seamstress.

A MEMORY
The Party

Is there a party from your past that stays in your mind? It could be one that was lots of fun—or perhaps it stands out because it wasn't any fun at all. Share your thoughts on the event, describing what you liked about it, or what you didn't like.

PREPLANNED FUNERAL

I have planned my funeral

Yes ☐   No ☐

I have paid for my funeral

Yes ☐   No ☐

I have chosen a burial plot

Yes ☐   No ☐

I have paid for a burial plot

Yes ☐   No ☐

Funeral Home

Name ....

Phone .... Email ....

Cemetery/Burial Plot

Name ....

Phone .... Email ....

Location of Funeral Agreement/Contract ....

Location of Cemetery Agreement/Contract ....

Tomb Stone/Memorial Stone

Chosen ☐   Prepaid ☐

Burial Outfit Preference ....

FUNERAL PLANS TO MAKE

Preference for Cremation ☐

Preference for Burial ☐

Preference for Burial Location ....
....
....

Preference for Tombstone/Memorial Stone   Yes ☐   No ☐

Tombstone/Memorial Stone Details ....
....
....

FUNERAL DETAILS

Flowers ☐   Preference ....
....
....
....

Music ☐   Preference ....
....
....
....

Readings ☐   Preference ....
....
....
....

Photos ☐   Preference ....
....
....
....

Other Preferences ....
....
....
....

FUNERAL OFFICIANTS

Arrangements Made ☐

Name of Officiant .... Phone ....

Name of Officiant .... Phone ....

Religious/Spiritual Leader ☐
Name .... Phone ....

Religious/Spiritual Leader ☐
Name .... Phone ....

Arrangements Not Made ☐

Preference for Officiants

Name of Officiant .... Phone ....

Name of Officiant .... Phone ....

Religious/Spiritual Leader ☐
Name .... Phone ....

Religious/Spiritual Leader ☐
Name .... Phone ....

MEMORIAL

Flowers ☐   Preference ....
....
....
....

Music ☐   Preference ....
....
....
....

Readings ☐   Preference ....
....
....
....

Photos ☐   Preference ....
....
....
....

Other Preferences ....
....
....
....

MEMORIAL OFFICIANTS

Preference for Officiants

Name of Officiant .... Phone ....

Name of Officiant .... Phone ....

Religious/Spiritual Leader ☐

Name .... Phone ....

Religious/Spiritual Leader ☐

Name .... Phone ....

TOMBSTONE/MEMORIAL STONE

Purchased ☐

Phone ....

Kind words are short and easy to speak, but their echoes are truly endless.

Mother Teresa

OBITUARY

I want an obituary ☐

I don't want an obituary ☐

I have written my obituary ☐

Location of Obituary ....

I want others to write my obituary ☐

Please Include:

Family ☐   My Profession ☐   My Interests ☐   Other ....

A CHARITY FOR DONATIONS ☐

My Preferred Charity ....

My Preferred Charity ....

My Preferred Charity ....

NOTIFICATION

Newspapers ☐

My Preferred Newspaper ....

Other ....

LITTLE-KNOWN FACTS

As we live our lives, there are events that we look back on with great pleasure or even a sense of pride or achievement. These small, often unrecognized, experiences of the past may not be shared unless a conversation jogs our memory. All the same, they can be savored and enjoyed by others.

If asked to reveal little-known facts about yourself, how would you answer? Think of a unique experience that you have had—a moment in time, such as a contest you entered or an unlikely adventure.

ADDITIONAL NOTES

LAST WISHES

REFLECTION

The words "last wishes" can be interpreted to mean many things. Some might interpret them as last wishes for others, for their community, or for the world. Others might express their last wishes as guidance to others based upon their own experiences.

We go through life gaining experiences that translate into lessons learned. Some cultures refer to this as wisdom. Some of us have lived longer years and through more stages of life, while others have faced greater challenges. We all have found ways to cope with the things life throws at us—from taking a walk in nature to seeking the support of friends and family. Your perspective is valuable. You are imparting a gift to others.

WHAT TO EXPECT

This section is personal. It asks you to share what you know and what you may have learned through the good times and the bad. It also allows you to express what is important to you, what you value, and to share experiences that are unique to you. Use this section of the book to record what you have learned over time about all the stages of life and to record what you have found to be helpful in meeting some of life's challenges.

HOW TO BEGIN

To complete this section, you will need a pen or a pencil and quiet time. Respond as the questions are relevant to you. I recommend that you go through this section in one sitting.

Use the additional notes page at the end of this section to list anything that isn't included. You can also use it as your own personal action list of things you need to return to in order to complete the information.

FIRSTS

I ventured from the city to a college campus in a small town surrounded by cornfields. I enjoyed the walkable downtown. Two diners, two pizza places, two barbers, a pharmacy, and a taxi service lined the street. On the edge of town were a variety of fast-food restaurants. Firsts for me. My first fast-food hamburger was the most delicious, decadent meal I had ever eaten. At home, my mother baked bread and cooked fresh vegetables, all underappreciated. That year, I looked forward to a mainstay of cola and crispy snacks while I studied. That year was also the first time I sat on bleachers and watched a football game. The dorm game room housed a ping-pong table. In my first game, and most games following, I'd swat the small plastic ball uncontrollably, sending it out of the room. Ping-pong thereafter became a fun nightly routine for many in the dorm. Eventually, the guys decided we needed a tournament. I added my name so that there would be enough players and a cheerleader for my friends. Snacks and cola in tow, I settled into a metal chair to wait my turn. My challenger was a friend against whom I had played many times. He practiced ball spins and slices and I would swat it predictably out of the room. Now, facing me once again, he sent the ball spinning toward me. I sent the ball back this time low and steady, time after time. Game after game the paddle seemed to have a life of its own, tapping the plastic ball, placing it in far corners of the table. Game after game, I remained. I returned to New York City as the ping-pong champion of my freshman year.

A MEMORY

Wishes

As children, many of us wish for things. We may want a particular toy or for some special event to happen. We are told about wishing on stars, or throwing a penny into a fountain, or blowing out our birthday candles. Do you recall something you wished for as a child? Share your memories here.

MEMORIES

BEFORE I WAS TEN YEARS OLD, I REMEMBER:

....

....

....

....

....

....

....

....

....

....

WHEN I WAS IN HIGH SCHOOL, I REMEMBER:

....

....

....

....

....

....

....

....

....

....

WHEN I WAS IN COLLEGE, I REMEMBER:

....

....

....

....

....

....

....

....

....

....

WHEN I WAS IN MY TWENTIES, I REMEMBER:

....

....

....

....

....

....

....

....

....

....

....

WHEN I WAS IN MY THIRTIES, I REMEMBER:

....

....

....

....

....

....

....

....

....

....

....

....

WHEN I WAS IN MY FORTIES, I REMEMBER:

....

....

....

....

....

....

....

....

....

....

....

....

WHEN I WAS IN MY FIFTIES, I REMEMBER:

....
....
....
....
....
....
....
....
....
....
....
....
....

WHEN I WAS IN MY SIXTIES, I REMEMBER:

....
....
....
....
....
....
....
....
....
....
....
....
....

WHEN I WAS IN MY SEVENTIES, I REMEMBER:

....
....
....
....
....
....
....
....
....
....
....
....

WHEN I WAS IN MY EIGHTIES, I REMEMBER:

....
....
....
....
....
....
....
....
....
....
....
....

OTHER MEMORIES:

....

....

....

....

....

....

....

....

....

....

....

....

....

....

....

....

....

....

....

....

....

....

....

....

....

MY WORK

Work can be defined in different ways throughout our lives. It is what we do every day or most days. Some of us work in the home or outside the home. Some of us have professions. Some of us have careers. Some of us have jobs.

MY FIRST JOB:

....

....

....

....

....

....

I LIKED IT BECAUSE:

....

....

....

....

....

....

I DIDN'T LIKE IT BECAUSE:

....

....

....

....

....

....

MY FAVORITE JOB:

....

....

....

....

....

....

....

....

....

....

I LIKED IT BECAUSE:

....

....

....

....

....

....

....

....

....

....

....

....

WHAT I HAVE ENJOYED ABOUT MY CAREER/PROFESSION:

....

....

....

....

....

....

....

....

....

....

....

OTHER THOUGHTS:

....

....

....

....

....

....

....

....

....

....

....

....

....

"I've come to believe that each of us has a personal calling that's as unique as a fingerprint."

Oprah Winfrey

LESSONS ON COPING

Think about what helps you when life is at its most challenging—something that gives you a sense of ease, well-being, or comfort. It can be one of many things. For some, it will be talking to a friend. For others, it will be sitting quietly. Others still may find participating in an activity offers distraction. We are all unique. How do you cope during hard times?

WHAT HELPS WHEN I FEEL ANGRY?

....

....

....

....

....

....

....

....

....

....

....

....

....

....

....

....

....

....

....

....

WHAT HELPS WHEN I FEEL ALONE?

WHAT HELPS WHEN I FEEL DISAPPOINTED?

WHAT HELPED WHEN SOMEONE I LOVED DIED?

....

....

....

....

....

....

....

....

....

....

....

....

....

....

....

....

....

....

....

....

....

....

....

....

....

....

....

You cannot swim for new horizons until you have courage to lose sight of the shore.

William Faulkner

WHAT I HOPE
FOR THE FUTURE

FOR MY FRIENDS:

....
....
....
....
....
....
....
....
....
....
....
....
....
....
....
....
....
....
....
....
....
....
....
....
....
....
....
....

FOR MY FAMILY:

FOR MY COLLEAGUES:

....
....
....
....
....
....
....
....
....
....
....
....
....
....
....
....
....
....
....
....
....
....
....
....
....
....
....
....
....

FOR MY COMMUNITY:

....

....

....

....

....

....

....

....

....

....

....

....

FOR THE WORLD:

....

....

....

....

....

....

....

....

....

....

....

....

....

To live in hearts we leave behind is not to die.

Thomas Campbell

WHAT I WANT YOU TO KNOW

None of us can be defined by a simple sentence.
We change constantly, often in small and simple ways. However,
what we believe to be true is often constant—the things we value in
others and in ourselves. Our principals, our sense of what is right
or wrong, rarely change in major ways.

Share the things that are true for you.

ADDITIONAL NOTES

Amy Levine is the Executive Director and Director of Education and Training for The Doula Program to Accompany and Comfort, a non-profit organization in New York City. Her work in end of life and serious illness has been recognized in publications such as *The New York Times*. She has been a contributing writer to the *Huffington Post* on her work with people at the end of life. Amy is a clinical social worker whose vast professional experience includes hospice and psychiatric services for older adults. She created the Palliative Care Doula Volunteer program which is used by major hospitals. In addition to her work with the Doula Program to Accompany and Comfort, she is an international consultant and speaker creating community workshops, professional training and health care programs. Contact Amy at: www.amylevineconsulting.com.

Brimming with creative inspiration, how-to projects, and useful information to enrich your everyday life, Quarto Knows is a favorite destination for those pursuing their interests and passions. Visit our site and dig deeper with our books into your area of interest: Quarto Creates, Quarto Cooks, Quarto Homes, Quarto Lives, Quarto Drives, Quarto Explores, Quarto Gifts, or Quarto Kids.

This edition published in 2021 by Rock Point, an imprint of The Quarto Group, 142 West 36th Street, 4th Floor, New York, NY 10018, USA

T (212) 779-4972 F (212) 779-6058

www.QuartoKnows.com

Rock Point titles are also available at discount for retail, wholesale, promotional, and bulk purchase. For details, contact the Special Sales Manager by email at specialsales@quarto.com or by mail at The Quarto Group, Attn: Special Sales Manager, 100 Cummings Center Suite 265D, Beverly, MA 01915 USA.

Designer: Josse Pickard

Editor: Emma Harverson

Publisher: Samantha Warrington

Printed in Singapore

This journal provides general information on grief and loss. It should not be relied upon as recommending or promoting any specific diagnosis or method of treatment for a particular condition, and it is not intended as a substitute for medical advice or for direct diagnosis and treatment of a medical condition by a qualified physician. Readers who have questions about a particular condition, possible treatments for that condition, or possible reactions from the condition or its treatment should consult a physician or other qualified healthcare professional.

ISBN: 978-1-63106-769-3

10 9 8 7 6 5 4 3 2 1